Table Of C

Preface / Introduction	2
Chapter 1: Understanding The Five Stages of Grief	5
Chapter 2: Exploring The Various Symptoms of Grief	13
Chapter 3: Self-Care During The Periods of Loss and Grief	18
Chapter 4: The Crucial Necessity of Emotional Support	24
Chapter 5: The Head On Approach To Facing Your Grief	31
Chapter 6: Accepting the Rocky Road Ahead of You	37
Chapter 7: Dealing With The Depression As A Result of Your Grief	41
Chapter 8: Complications of Grief & How To Overcome Them	49
Chapter 9: The Importance of Patience and Forgiveness	54
Chapter 10: Seeing The Silver Lining and Learning To Appreciate Life	60
Final Thoughts and Further Insight	66
Stories	68

Preface / Introduction

There is nothing more painful than suffering from grief.

Whether it's caused by the death of a loved one or the ending of a very important relationship, grief can be one of the largest hurdles a person must overcome.

Fortunately, there are ways that you can begin to move on from the most crippling elements of grief so that you may begin to live your life again.

It may seem impossible, but if you're devoted to your healing, then there's nothing that can stop you from moving forward in your life and taking something valuable away from your experiences.

It can be very difficult to come face to face with the loss of a loved one or valuable relationship, but there's always some kind of silver lining that can be found, no matter what the difficulty faced might be. It can take a lot of time to recover, so try to be patient with yourself during the process.

Although there are bound to be times when the pain seems overwhelming, the truth is that humans are adaptable creatures who can heal and move forward with grace and wisdom from even the most tragic of events. Natural disasters and wars have left many people in shambles, but with time and dedication, even the most devastated can begin to find solace and healing.

But with some time and a few tricks in changing our perspective, we can begin to live again instead of sinking further into the depths of depression that can so easily consume us during times of grief.

Losing a loved one or cherished relationship can be unbelievably difficult, but if you're dedicated to holding on to the things that are important, you should be able to move forward no matter how hard it may seem.

What's really crucial is that you don't give up on yourself and you provide yourself with the patience you need to go through the stages of grieving that allow us to begin to prime ourselves for the healing process.

This course will help you to gain the information necessary in moving forward from a tragic experience so that you can reclaim your life and overcome grief, no matter what the source.

Angels are always near to those who are grieving.
To whisper to them that their loved ones are safe in the hands of God.

Chapter 1 : Understanding The Five Stages of Grief

Grief is a complex cycle that comes with many stages and separate experiences that can keep us overwhelmed by the complexities of dealing with the loss of a significant relationship or situation.

It can be very scary for somebody who has never experienced grief to be stuck in the different stages of their grieving, and it can make them volatile and hostile.

Everybody grieves in different ways, and may not even experience the stages of grief in the same order. However, what can be agreed upon is that despite how difficult it may seem for us to move forward once we have been unexpectedly hit with the difficulties of a significant loss is that at some point, we will find our peace with acceptance.

Unfortunately, this is usually the last stage of grief that we arrive at, and we can quickly jump from acceptance right back to denial and back again. Grief is tricky and can take quite a while for us to process.

The biggest thing we can do to help ourselves through this process is to understand as much about grief as we possibly can and be patient and forgiving of ourselves as we deal with the issues that are frequently associated with grieving and loss.

Chances are high that if you're reading this book, you're probably suffering from a fresh loss. However, there's also a possibility that you have suffered a loss that only feels fresh, and has actually occurred a significant time ago. And truthfully, only you can determine whether a loss feels new or not.

The pain from your loss can last a lifetime. However, it shouldn't cripple you or keep you from adapting to your new circumstances. There is a time when it's more important to begin to move forward with your life than to dwell on the past, no matter how deeply felt your loss may have been.

Whether you're having trouble moving forward after a loss that has occurred or you're struggling to deal with fresh feelings of grief from an unexpectedly difficult loss, this course was designed to help you to understand the grieving process better, and help you to overcome the debilitating symptoms that can so easily make us lose track of the things that are important in our own lives. If we become too consumed by our grief, we may lose sight of the things that make living our lives so rewarding.

Taking this course shows that you're already aware of the responsibilities that you have toward yourself and your own healing. That is a step that's very admirable and it takes a lot of inner strength and courage. If you're having a hard time with your grief, that can often times be difficult simply to articulate and admit, let alone seeking resources to help you. Congratulations on making it this far! You are stronger than you think you are.

Now, let's start to discuss the five stages of grief. The stage that often comes first is **Denial**. When we hear the horrible news, our automatic response is to deny what we have heard because we do not want to accept that it's true. We don't even want to think that it could be possible. When we're confronted with a terrible situation that feels much more like a nightmare than it feels like our reality, we want to run and hide as far away from that reality as possible. This is when we go into denial.

It can be a very trying stage for you, as well as other people who are connected to the situation but may be experiencing different stages of the grief cycle. When you're feeling like the news you have just heard is too terrible to be true and you check out of reality for a little while, it can be frustrating to others who are angry about the loss or depressed about the loss to reiterate the fact that yes, it really is happening and there's nothing more to be said or done about it, no matter how hard you try.

The next stage of grief is **Anger**. When things hurt us unexpectedly, it's pretty common that we get angry about it. We don't want to just lie down and take it when things are painful. Usually there's someone alive and malicious out there who is causing us harm, so our natural reflex seems to be anger. Whether we're angry at the subject of our loss for leaving or angry at others for how they are treating the loss, the end feeling is the same.

When we're angry at our loss, we're generally asking ourselves why such a terrible thing has happened to us. It may feel unfair, undeserved, and agitating to know that we're suering for some unknown reason, or even for no reason whatsoever. But our minds need to try to make sense of everything that happens to us, and when we can't find the correlation between cause and effect, that can make us feel helpless, which makes us feel even more angry.

We like to be in control. And losing control never feels very good, especially when what we're trying to control is out of our hands. Things like death can be especially infuriating when we're trying to maintain structure and control in our lives.

The third stage of grief is **Bargaining**. Bargaining occurs when we have allowed the idea of the loss to sink in for a few moments, but it's still so profoundly difficult for us to handle that we feel we will do anything to reverse the negative effects of the situation we're in.

We will make promises we can't keep and offer to be completely different or better people if some higher power with more control than we have will just take mercy upon us.

When we're swept up in grief, we often feel like we would do anything possible to make the bad feelings that we're having go away. Unfortunately, most of the time loss that inspires grief is irreversible.

Sure, we may grieve the loss of a friendship or relationship that could eventually be repaired if both parties are mature enough, but a lot of the time when we grieve, it's because of events beyond our control that can't be reversed. When we're grieving a death for example, it's impossible to reverse the effects. We can make any promises to the powers that be that we can think of, but it still will not change the end result of our loss.

The fourth stage of grief, and often the most long-lasting and common stage, is **Depression**. When we're dealing with the results of grief in our lives, it can be easy to sink into a state of depression and unhappiness that can leave us immobile. Depression is a state that can freeze us, and prevent us from moving forward. If we get stuck too long into painful states of depression, we may lose sight of what makes life worth living, and begin to degrade our quality of life.

Depression is difficult to move through because we don't want to move at all. Most of the time, depression leaves us slow and unmotivated. We would rather lie in bed and feel terrible than get up and do the things that are expected of us and sometimes that's okay. It can be what we need to take a break from the responsibilities of our everyday lives so that we can take the time we need to begin to mentally and emotionally process our loss.

However, it can be a slippery slope. Sure, we can justify being depressed for a week or two after a shocking loss, but if that depression persists for too long it can become a chronic state that will be discussed in a later section. Chronic depression can all but destroy our lives and the stability that we struggle to build, and if we allow ourselves to dwell in this dangerous emotional state, it can have lasting consequences.

Fortunately, while we're grieving, the depression stage doesn't always throw us for a loop. We can be depressed in a healthy way and allow ourselves to process the difficult emotions that are plaguing us. If we allow ourselves to move successfully through the individual stages of grief, even if we skip a few (or even all of them) and make it to acceptance of the situation relatively unscathed, then we will not have to worry about depression impacting us for the rest of our lives. But because this stage of grief can be so all-encompassing, it will be discussed more in depth later in the course.

The final stage of depression is **Acceptance**. Acceptance can be something that we need to work very hard for, especially when we're struggling through the other four stages of grief. It may take quite a few cycles before we reach a permanent state of acceptance. A lot of people might think that the cycles of grief are an easy list that we all experience one by one in perfect order until we reach the end, but unfortunately that's not the case. There are many times when acceptance cannot be reached permanently until the cycles of grief have been experienced several times over, sometimes very out of order.

But that is okay, because we're all individuals who require different emotional processes before we're able to move forward with our lives. Emotions can be very complicated and it isn't wrong of us to take our time to process feelings that are extremely difficult. Eventually we will arrive at acceptance, even if it takes a while.

When we are able to reach acceptance of the difficulty of our loss, then we find ourselves at peace with what has happened to us. That doesn't mean that thinking about it won't cause us pain. In fact, sometimes the loss of a loved one will pain us always. But we can go from being so overwhelmed by grief when we think of them to finally being able to smile and remember the wonderful things about having them in our lives, even if we're smiling through our tears.

Acceptance simply means that we are at peace with the fact that the loss has happened, and in finding that peace we're able to move on from the overwhelming and seemingly insurmountable grief in order to continue living our lives to the best of our abilities. When we're able to cope with our loss, then we're able to move forward and continue to create harmony and peace in other aspects of our lives.

WHEN WE LOSE *someone* WE

love

WE MUST LEARN

not to live without them,

BUT TO LIVE WITH THE LOVE

they left

behind.

- ANONYMOUS

Chapter 2: Exploring The Various Symptoms of Grief

Sometimes, before we can heal we have to know precisely how it is that we are suffering. Grief can often times leave us reeling, as it's always fairly surprising when we encounter a loss that we don't expect. Even when we expect a loss, experiencing it is much different than anticipating it. We often aren't prepared for the wild emotions that rise up during times of strife.

Understanding the symptoms of grief will help you to navigate your relationships responsibly during your time of loss and help you to feel more patient with yourself as you go through this difficult time in your life.

It is normal when experiencing a difficult loss to feel sad. Sometimes this sadness can be so profound and overwhelming that it takes you by surprise and makes you wish that you could have some sense of control over it. You may ache and yearn for feelings and situations that were once commonplace in your life but will now no longer be an option because of the loss you have experienced.

Crying is a normal and healthy aspect of experiencing a loss, and if you feel like crying then it's okay to allow yourself to do so. Whether you want to feel sadness or not, if you feel it washing over you it's all right to let it.

In fact, crying is a very important and healthy thing to do for your body, and this will be discussed later on in a different section. Sadness is normal and it can be common to feel as if you're experiencing a state of instability during grieving. We can even find ourselves dealing with uncommonly extreme emotions, the strongest of which may be despair, loneliness, or even emptiness. Sadness is an all-encompassing emotion that can be complex and dicult to sort out, but it's also a symptom of grief, and one that's the most common.

Fortunately, sadness is simply one range of human emotion, and once you have finished experiencing it you can move on to another feeling entirely. Crying when you're sad makes your body physically more prone to experiencing feelings of pleasure and happiness, so don't feel guilty if your sadness gives way to something more peaceful. Nothing you feel during your time of grief is wrong. But what can be wrong is to dwell needlessly in sadness or use it as an excuse to act upon inappropriate emotions. Overall, sadness is a common symptom of grief and should be allowed to wash over you until the power of the sadness has waned with the experience of going through the different stages of grief.

Another common symptom of a grieving person is being in a perpetual state of disbelief. We don't like being faced with unpleasant realities like the death of a loved one or the loss of a significant relationship. Before we've gotten used to the bad news, we might find ourselves expecting to see the person who is gone or experience emotions from situations that will no longer affect us. When we first hear the news it's common to go into denial, and symptoms of denial may be extended as you continue on through the grieving process.

One of the worst symptoms of grief that we can experience is guilt. Guilt can wreak havoc on our lives and leave us immobile when we should be trying to move on from the bad experience. Instead of moving on, however, we can be tortured with guilt and constantly worrying over whether or not we did something wrong. Maybe we're worried about what we didn't say or do, or maybe we're too worried about the way that things we did say or do were perceived by someone else, especially when the loss we're experiencing is the death of a loved one.

However, these kinds of regrets lead nowhere fast, and you will have to learn to let go of that guilt if you want to move forward on your healing journey. There will be more to come on that subject in a later section.

Other symptoms of grief include anger and fear. Anger and fear are closely related emotions. When we're afraid, we become angry, and when we're angry, it's often because we're afraid. When we lose someone that we love, it's common to begin to feel resentful. Perhaps you think that there are ways that the person we love could have been saved, whether by you or by somebody else.

Maybe you can think of hundreds of different ways the situation could have been avoided, and you're angry that nobody else was smart enough to avoid the worst-case scenario in your loved one's life. Sometimes we're even angry at the person we lost, whether they could help their circumstances or not. None of us like to feel like we have been left behind.

If you're feeling fearful, that's also understandable and a common symptom of grief. Grieving has a tendency to make us feel like the worst things in the depths of our imaginations can come into being, and it can even make us feel afraid to be happy in case that happiness is taken away as suddenly as the security of the loved one or situation that we're grieving was taken from us. Some people develop anxiety and panic attacks when they are dealing with the profound effects of grief. It is common to feel this way, although it might be useful to seek professional help if your fears begin to get the better of you.

Often these anxieties and fears will dissipate over time, but sometimes we carry with us the burden of knowing that nothing is certain. If one bad thing could happen, other bad things could happen. While this may be true, it's no way to allow yourself to live. Fearing the next moment makes it impossible for us to enjoy the present. Whether we are afraid for our own lives and mortality or we're afraid that we cannot hold onto the good things in our lives, it's always best not to let your anxieties take control. If they do, then there are many qualified people out there who can help you to process your anxieties and proceed to help you to take control back over your own life.

There will come a day when
the tears of sorrow will softly flow
into tears of remembrance...
and your heart will begin
to heal itself...
and grieving will be interrupted
by episodes of joy
and you will hear the whispers of hope.
There will come a day
when you will welcome
the tears of remembrance...
as a sun-shower of the soul...
a turning of the tide...
a promise of peace. There will
come a day when you will
risk loving
go on believing
and treasure the
tears of remembrance

Chapter 3: Self-Care During The Periods of Loss and Grief

Back in the old days, it was common to visit your friends and neighbors during times of loss with food and dishes to leave for them. This tradition began because of the common tendency that people in grieving have toward losing interest in their own self-care.

When we are grieving, it can be difficult to maintain the lifestyle that we're used to. We don't feel hunger the same way we once did, and we lack a drive to take care of ourselves the ways we once were able to do so easily. It is difficult for us sometimes to find the motivation we need to cook and clean and go out to find comfort in our friends and communities as a whole. And this sad reality is why it became so commonplace for neighbors to reach out to their grieving neighbors and friends with gifts of food. Sometimes people would even check in on them and help with a bit of housework.

If you notice other people trying to come to you with offers of this type of help, try not to take it the wrong way. As a community, most of us understand that the death of a loved one or the loss of a significant relationship can be a difficult experience. We sink into depression, and even if we don't notice ourselves caring less about the things we should, other people are sure to know the difference. If you're having trouble caring for yourself during a loss, there's no shame in accepting help from others.

However, extended grief that becomes unhealthy and dependent on other people should be closely examined and monitored. Don't indulge your grief more than you have to, but also take care to be honest with yourself about how you're feeling. If you're feeling up to taking care of yourself, do it. Don't wait for someone to tell you that it's what you should do. Take the initiative yourself.

But if you don't even notice yourself falling into disrepair, take advice from friends and family members. If someone is telling you that you should eat, listen to them. Let them cook for you and help you out with the cleaning a little bit. Sometimes this can help us to feel more inspired to take care of ourselves, no matter how glum we might be feeling at the time. A lot of people don't like accepting help from others, even when they need it. But when you're grieving, there's no shame in it at all.

Self-care can be very difficult during trying times. Grief can make it seem nearly impossible to notice or care about all the tiny aspects that go into successful day-to-day living. Unfortunately, there comes a time when we have to get back on the horse. Even if we don't feel like it, we have to take into account the things we need to do daily in order to keep ourselves healthy and strong. If we don't, then the grieving process will become exceedingly overwhelming and you may just find yourself sinking further and further into a pit of depression that you can't escape.

This is why it's especially important to stay on top of your self-care. Even though you may have taken care of yourself without a second thought before experiencing grief, you may need the help of some tools while you're experiencing the grieving process. You should keep a journal with a to-do list in it so that every morning you can cross off the items that you have done in order to take care of yourself. Be diligent about this, as it's extremely important to make sure that you're keeping yourself and your body in the best shape it can possibly be in. If you neglect your health, then you're making it harder for yourself to heal from the emotional wounds that you're trying to recover from.

Another thing you can do is to have some accountability to somebody else. This serves two purposes. First of all, it ensures that you're not retreating into your own little shell as you grieve. Socializing and having a support network is more important than most of us realize. The second thing it does is to help us think about the things we need to do and inspire us to do them. It can be embarrassing to have a friend ask us, "did you brush your teeth today?" and answer "no."

If you know you're going to be held accountable for having done your self-care ritual and you'll have to answer embarrassing questions, chances are high that you'll think ahead and act accordingly so you can answer "yes" to people questioning whether or not you have been taking proper care of yourself.

If you don't have somebody who would be able to hold you accountable in that way, that's all right. We can work hard on our own to maintain our self-care routines. It will take extra effort to get through them while we're grieving, but if you constantly remind yourself why it's important that you exercise self-care during trying times, you will succeed.

You could recite a mantra daily as soon as you wake up to help you to prepare yourself for the day ahead. You could say something like, "Whether I like it or not, I have to take care of myself, and so today I will." Listing some of the things that you need to do may be especially beneficial during the morning, while you're preparing yourself both mentally and physically for the day ahead. If you feel yourself wavering throughout the day, just remember your mantra and try to draw power from it.

If a journal isn't practical enough, having a dry-erase board in place where you can easily see it can be helpful. Just write a checklist of the things you need to accomplish during the day that you're having trouble with during the grieving process and check them off as you complete them.

Taking care of yourself first and foremost is the most important thing you can do while you're grieving. If you don't take care of your basic needs, then everything else is going to seem much more difficult than it has to be. When we aren't taking care of ourselves, we know it, and our bodies respond accordingly. We want to withdraw even further from others because we are not in our prime state, physically and mentally, and it can often lead to isolation and depression. We feel good when we're clean and well-fed. When we're not, it makes us surly, angry, irritable, and depressed.

The importance of self-care during times of grief cannot be understated. Nobody is going to be able to take care of you as well as you're able to take care of yourself. For that reason, it's essential that you do everything in your power to make sure that all of your most basic needs are met as you continue to move through the difficult transition ahead of you.

But don't worry, it doesn't always feel so difficult. It may seem hard now, but as time wears on, self-care becomes easier and will soon be something you want to do. But staying in the habit right in the thick of things is the most important thing you can do for yourself. Even if you have to use tricks and tools like the ones stated above, making sure that you're in the best state you can possibly be in will be essential in keeping your physical and emotional self strong enough to endure the challenges that lie ahead as you work to overcome grief.

*Keep your head up.
God gives his hardest battles
to his strongest soldiers.*

Chapter 4: The Crucial Necessity of Emotional Support

It would be ill-advised to try to embark upon overcoming grief alone. In fact, sometimes it can be almost impossible to do so. Grieving may be a very personal thing that nobody else in the world can understand, but having a support network when things get tough is unbelievably important.

When the going gets tough, a lot of the times we tend to retreat from our communities, and cut ourselves off from the crucial support of our social structures and peer groups. Friends and family members are forced to worry about us from afar, and we no longer feel up to socializing the way we once had. But this state of mind can be very dangerous.

Without the social support we once had, we can often become very comfortable in our isolation. It becomes easy for us to convince ourselves that nobody really understands, and because nobody really understands, then nobody can really care about us or what we are experiencing. That can make us bitter and resentful of any social interactions that we might have, especially when the people reaching out to us truly seem baffled by our experiences or they are made uncomfortable by our strong emotions.

However, try not to be so quick to judge others for being uncomfortable when dealing with grief. It is a profound and complicated process that can sometimes change our lives forever, so if our social group is having a hard time guring out how to approach us, it isn't because they don't care. They simply are not you and have never been in the exact position you're in right that moment.

Instead of trying to push them away, instead, inform them of the things that you need so that they can assist you appropriately. It would be hasty to cut them out just because they don't have the proper words to express their desire to do whatever they can to help you through the difficult time you're having. Once they know how they can help, they are happy to do so.

It can be really difficult for us to ask for and accept help when we need it, but when we're grieving, for some reason, reaching out to others seems to be the hardest thing we can possibly do. We want to be alone to wallow in our misery. We want to be allowed to cut ourselves off from human contact and withdraw from other situations and relationships that might carelessly put salt in our wounds.

We want to protect ourselves from more pain, and we don't always want to be cared for by people who just don't understand what we're dealing with or how we feel. And really, there's nothing wrong with feeling that way. You are entitled to some alone time during the grieving process.

However, the support of other people can be very important. Grief can turn us into people we didn't know we could be. We can have extreme emotions and outbursts that we don't mean. We might lash out at others or take things the wrong way because we're feeling vulnerable and raw. And so it makes sense that we withdraw. It makes sense that we don't want to surround ourselves with people we might hurt, who might hurt us, when none of us mean to hurt each other at all. The ironic thing about this is that without the support of others, the isolation we find comfort in can become permanent.

None of us want to be alone forever, no matter how tempting it might sound. We might not see how silly and irrational we're acting until someone else points it out. We might not remember to do things that are important to our self-care rituals if someone doesn't remind us. We might not realize that although we feel very alone, what we sometimes really need to do is talk to somebody about how we feel, whether they can understand and relate to us or not. Sometimes, all we really need is a hug and reassurance that even though it feels impossible, things are going to turn out all right.

As much as we might feel like being alone is helping us to heal, in truth, the support of other people is what we need the most during times of grief. Although it can seem difficult and unwanted, being around your community and being part of a group of people who truly care about you can help you to speed up the healing that you need during a time of loss.

Other people offer emotional support and kindness when you may be feeling cynical and angry. Having this kind of support during grieving can be like a balm over painful emotional wounds. Not only that, but allowing other people into your life can help you to get out of the house and into new situations where you're forced to face life and interact with others instead of being pulled deeper and deeper into your own grief.

That can be especially good, especially if you're naturally inclined toward shyness or retreating into an inner world where others are not invited. When you're forced to face life and react to external events, the stages of grief seem to go a little more smoothly, at least that's true if you keep good company. However, it's important not to make the mistake of surrounding yourself with people who will deplete you.

For example, you don't want to have emotional support from people who are inconsiderate and selfish, who care more about themselves and petty problems than they care about being there for a friend in need. Be careful when choosing who to spend your time with, because it's just as bad to spend time with the wrong people as it is to avoid emotional support from others altogether.

Now that you know what kinds of people to avoid, here are some people that you can turn to during times of need. Most of the time, these are people who will help you and offer you the emotional support that you need to stay on a path of healing.

Family members and friends are great sources of emotional support. It can be helpful to stay close to other people who may be experiencing the same loss or same type of loss as you're experiencing, but remember that these people are also consumed by their own stages of grief and may not always be available to support you in the way that you need. Regardless, there's nothing quite like being close to people who are dealing with a similar tragedy as you're dealing with and being there for each other can be truly miraculous.

On this same end, support groups full of survivors and other people who are working through grief can be an amazing source of emotional support. Other people who are experiencing the same types of problems as you're dealing with can share insights into the ways they have been able to get over similar hurdles and challenges in their grieving process. They will also understand your loss in ways that other people who are not experiencing loss cannot. It is a wonderful way to find validation in your emotions and make great friends who can truly understand how you feel in a way other people will not always be able to.

There is also the option of seeking counselling from a certified grief counsellor or therapist. Sometimes this can be the best way to help us sort through our emotions during times that are overwhelming and difficult for us. There can be many challenges that we face during the grieving process, and fortunately counsellors are experts in emotions and working through problems like this. Make sure you trust and like your therapist enough to form a relationship with them and talk about personal things with them, otherwise it will not necessarily be as rewarding an experience as you might hope for.

A lot of people are also able to find emotional support from their religious institutions. If you follow any type of spiritual practice, seeking comfort in the guidance that your faith might offer can be a great way to find emotional support. It is highly likely that organizations of your faith will have services to offer you during times of need, and utilizing these resources can be a great way to strengthen your faith and form bonds with like-minded people who want to help you move through the grieving process.

No matter where you find your emotional support, what's really important is that you hold on to it even when times prove to be difficult and challenging. Overcoming grief can be a huge issue in your life, but with the right people, sharing the burden can make it that much easier for you to move on and begin healing.

Grief, I've learned, is really just love. It's all the love you want to give, but cannot. All of that unspent love gathers in the corners of your eyes, the lump in your throat, and in the hollow part of your chest. *Grief is just love with no place to go.*

-Jamie Anderson

Chapter 5: The Head On Approach To Facing Your Grief

A common mistake that people who are grieving often make is that they are unable or unwilling to face their grief head-on. How do you face grief head-on? The first thing you do is to stay in the present moment without allowing yourself to retreat into the recesses of your mind. It means making an active effort not to dwell in your own sorrow. It means realizing that grieving, although an important process, is not the be-all end-all of your relationship with the person or thing that you lost.

Grieving, in fact, is more like the proof that you had something meaningful in your life and you are capable of giving and receiving love. Some people say that grieving is all the love that we have for someone or something without being able to give it to them. Since it has nowhere to go, it stays in us and makes us sad.

However you choose to look at grief, the fact remains that we don't get anywhere by burying our heads in the sand and letting the world fall apart around us. It is our responsibility to keep it together, no matter what's happening in our lives. Whether it feels insurmountable or not, if we aren't courageous enough to look grief in the eye and accept that this is a normal and natural experience, we're going to have a more difficult time in healing. If we don't face grief head-on, it becomes a long, tedious process that can harm us and the people we love for years to come.

If you choose to avoid feeling your sad feelings because grief seems too painful to deal with, the chances are high that you're creating much deeper problems for yourself further on down the line. Although grief can be overwhelming and difficult, it should be experienced in all of its miserable splendor. Trying to hide from it will only impact the symptoms and make them worse.

When you're having a hard time accepting your emotions, they can affect you in ways you can't control. Repressing feelings can make them come out more aggressively than you mean for them to. It can drive away the people you love and cause confusions and miscommunication that doesn't need to occur. Trying to act like you're fine when truly you're grieving is detrimental to your emotional health, and not only that but it's dishonest. Nobody expects you to be ne after suffering a terrible loss, so being honest about how you feel is not only a relief for you, but a relief to people who don't want you to lie to them because you think that it's what they want to hear.

Even if it's easier to shut out the pain, doing so is not healthy. It can lead to some serious complications in the grieving process, which we'll cover in a later section. These complications can impact every aspect of your life and make it seem impossible to move on without the person or thing that you're grieving. It can cause you to become stuck in a time of anguish when processing your feelings will provide you with an opportunity to heal and begin to live your life again.

Sure, it's intimidating, but the truth is that each and every one of us have the strength and courage necessary to slay the beast. We simply have to stay aware of ourselves and our strengths and weaknesses, just like any other hero. If you're honest about your shortcomings then you can begin to embrace solutions.

So you're having an issue with accepting grief as a part of your life? Do you think it makes you seem weaker to allow yourself to grieve properly? Are the feelings seemingly too insurmountable to even think about? Whatever the reason it seems difficult to brave the hurdles that grief has thrown in front of you, there are ways around them and finding these ways is necessary and crucial to your mental and emotional health.

The first step is being honest with ourselves. This is something big and scary, probably unlike anything we have ever experienced before. It's all right to be afraid. It's all right to be angry and to want to hide from it. But it's wrong to hide. The unfortunate fact is that life has changed and we must allow ourselves to process these changes so that we can begin to adjust. Otherwise, we'll stay in a constant state of imbalance, not allowing ourselves the proper time that we need to adjust to the radical changes that have shocked our lives. We may suppress the symptoms of grief that we're naturally inclined to experience.

This can bring on a whole variety of issues, from inexplicable and seemingly irrational fears to anxiety or depressive disorders that can impact your life in negative ways. Many people even turn to substance abuse to try to numb their pain, which can easily turn into addictions that take over their lives. It's very dangerous to deny your negative feelings, and even if it feels too big and difficult to deal with alone, remember that you're not alone. There is help for those who seek it.

We have to admit that we were impacted and that these impacts were negative. We have to be kind to ourselves even if other people seem impatient with the symptoms of our grief. People who may not be experiencing the same type of loss as you are and people who may never have experienced that type of loss are likely to say things that make you cringe or imply that you're dealing incorrectly with your emotions. Some people will tell you that it's time to move on early in your grieving process. But trying to rush your healing because of advice from someone who isn't experienced with grief can actually hurt us more than it helps us.

It is up to us to face the difficulties of our grieving process, or risk ever being able to move forward in our lives. You could try to keep a journal if you're not comfortable talking about all of the difficult emotions that you're experiencing, so that every day you can express how you're feeling about your loss. You could try talking to a professional who is qualified in helping people to cope with losses like the one you're experiencing. You can confide in a trusted friend or loved one, you can use art as a therapeutic device to begin to process the difficult emotions, and you can even try to play music.

However it is you begin to cope with the devastating effects of your loss, it's the right way. It is a step toward healing, no matter how difficult it may have been to take it. And you are strong and courageous enough to begin to take control of your life, no matter how difficult it might be. Just believe in yourself and don't let anyone invalidate your emotions. Coping with your grief is crucial.

Never Forgotten

I think of things you used to say
And all that you would do,
At some point, every single day,
My thoughts will turn to you.

To lose you was a bitter wrench,
The pain cut to my core.
I cried until my tears ran out
And then I cried some more.

This wouldn't be your wish for me
That I'd be forever sad
So I try to remind myself
Of the happy times we had.

I know I can't be with you now
And you can't be with me
But safe inside my heart you'll stay,
That's where you'll always be.

Chapter 6: Accepting the Rocky Road Ahead of You

The fact is that life has changed. Something that you used to rely on as a constant in your life has been removed. It has now become a variable that may never be part of your life again, except in the ways that you still have control over, such as through prayers or rituals to honor those we have lost. But often, the little bit of control we have left is not enough.

There are many methods for dealing with death and loss, but they might all seem to pale in comparison to having the actual person or relationship back in your life. You may even be grieving a loss of security. Maybe before a tragedy you once felt safe, but now that you know such bad things can happen, you find it more difficult to feel confident that such things may not happen to you again, maybe even more directly.

These are common occurrences when one is dealing with grief, but if you have allowed yourself to begin to process the difficult and complicated stages of grief in your own life, you're going to have to begin to look at your life in a new way. There is something unhappy that we have to accept. Things are never going to be the same. We don't like it. We don't want to accept it. It hurts to believe it. But that's the fact of the matter, and we have to face it despite how hard it might be.

Allowing yourself to experience grief can be difficult, and it can be more difficult to accept the full implications of our loss. Fortunately there are things that we can do to make the transition easier. We can write letters to the people we have lost outlining things that may still be lingering on our minds. If there are words and feelings that were left unsaid, say them in a letter to the person you've lost. You may find unexpected closure from the act.

Sometimes it can help to plan memorials and find support of other people through your communities. These types of events can be helpful to plan through social media and other cornerstones of your community, such as through religious and spiritual organizations that hope to help people cope with emotional difficulties. Many people find comfort and healing in turning their energies toward causes that are related to their loss. For example, if the person they have lost died of cancer, they will find comfort and peace championing the cause by organizing fundraisers so they can donate money to seek the cure.

It is also important to remember that there will be times throughout your life, possibly forever, that you're made vulnerable by the memory of your loss. The people that we love who are no longer with us can leave a profound lasting effect on us, and it's only natural that we feel sad sometimes, especially during significant anniversaries and holidays that remind us of them. We can take these opportunities to celebrate the lives of our loved ones and make special efforts to show love and honor the people we have lost.

It's completely normal, even after the grieving process has rested with acceptance, to have extremely difficult times during these anniversaries and holidays. It's best to be honest with everybody about how you're feeling and why, so that they can make efforts to honor your feelings, no matter what they may be. They may want to honor your loved one right alongside you, and you can discuss different ways to include the person you're grieving into your ceremonies and holidays as you deem appropriate.

If you can look into the future and see times when you might be vulnerable or have some emotional difficulty, don't keep it to yourself. Tell the people in your life so they can begin to give you the space and comfort that you need in order to maintain your balance. It's perfectly fine to be sad and to grieve during these times. Just make sure to remember the importance of self-care during these times and do what you need in order to feel comfortable.

Little by little, we let go of loss... but never of love.

Chapter 7: Dealing With The Depression As A Result of Your Grief

Depression is a natural aspect of the grieving process, and in fact it's one of the main stages of grief. Unfortunately, depression can become complicated quickly and it can lead to some issues that can easily become life-altering, and not in a positive way.

One thing that can quickly push us into depression is the ingrained expectation that during times of grief, there's no opportunity for happiness and joy. We may feel angry at ourselves for feeling positive during times we think we should only feel dark and miserable. While it's true that you have lost somebody special to you, it's not wrong to allow yourself to feel little bits of joy and pleasure.

If we punish ourselves for feeling positively during times of grief, our grieving can quickly turn into depression. And depression is all-encompassing. It isn't the same as the brief states of depression we feel during the five stages of grief. Depression is longer lasting and can seriously impede our progress in life. Don't punish yourself for being able to be positive during the rollercoaster of emotions that define the grieving process. Falling into a chronic depression is much worse. Your loved one would not want you to suffer in this way.

It is a mistake to take antidepressants during the initial stages of the grieving process, as it simply numbs the symptoms but not the cause of your grief. Ironically enough, it can make the grieving process last even longer because it's just another way to try to hide from your negative feelings without allowing yourself to accept the difficulty of the situation. As mentioned before, it's always best to face your grief head-on, without attempting to hide from the feelings or numb them through drugs, even if they are prescribed by a well-meaning physician.

Much of the time it's hard to tell grief and depression apart. Fortunately, there are some telling signs that will tell you when you're beginning to deal with clinical depression rather than simply grieving. One way to know is if you have been grieving for several years after the loss that occurred. Somewhere along the way, the grieving process may have become quite complicated and your attempts to process your emotions may have been distorted by depression. This is common and generally referred to as complicated grief, which will be discussed in the next section.

Depression is different from grief in several ways. For example, if you have excessive feelings of guilt, much more so than you did in the beginning stages of your grieving process, it can be caused by depression. You may begin to feel guilty about things that are in no way your fault, whether they are connected to the one you lost or not. These complications can make it feel impossible to move on when you're trying to cope with life, because you begin to get stuck in a deep well of self-loathing.

Feeling excessive guilt can cause you to begin to wonder why you cannot do anything right. You may have your entire world experience clouded by these insurmountable feelings of guilt that can lead to some serious issues with your relationship with yourself and with others as well. It can lead you deeper into isolation because you become too afraid of hurting others the way you feel you may have hurt the one you loved and lost. But these guilty feelings are completely irrational. Even if they seem to have a firm logical foundation, the fact is that humans are much stronger than you're giving them credit for. Even if you hurt their feelings a little bit, chances are high they will bounce back from it without hating your guts. The chances are even higher if you apologize.

But depression plays tricks with our minds and convinces us that we're terrible human beings unworthy of social connections, and the intense guilt we feel is justified because we're terrible. However, that is not true, and allowing yourself to be swept into the guilt introduced by grief is a huge mistake. But it can be unavoidable if you have fallen into depression. Just try to remember it's your mind playing tricks on you and take control in the ways that you can without isolating yourself.

Another symptom of depression that is different from grief, is a preoccupation with death. More specifically, a preoccupation with your own death, whether it be by suicide or other factors beyond our control. Maybe you become more afraid of dying, or you feel so terrible it feels like dying may serve as the only conceivable relief.

However, that's untrue and it should be seen for what it is. Depression can introduce many horrible thoughts to us, whether we feel good about ourselves at the beginning of the grieving process or not.

Grief can warp our perspective, and depression can change it even further and convince us with false logic that we're worthless and that there's no hope. Depression is an extremely dangerous state to be in, especially during or after a profound loss, so if you're worried that you're suffering from feelings of depression please speak to somebody. There is help for you if you ask for it. Only you know your personal experience.

Other symptoms of depression include a difficulty in functioning at home, school, or work. These issues can lead to many problems, especially if you're a teenager with your whole life ahead of you or if you're in the middle of something important that you need to make progress with. The complications of this sort of grief can be unbelievably detrimental, and if they aren't dealt with quickly, they can set your life on a dark course that can seem insurmountable.

Sometimes, people with depression even hallucinate. It can be commonplace for people with depression to see or hear things that aren't there, especially when those things concern aspects of themselves that they feel insecure or unhappy about. Depression is quite a dangerous state to be in, and if you're suffering from any symptoms of depression, it's important that you speak to somebody about it.

One final symptom of depression that is separate from the symptoms of grief is slow movements. People who have a tendency to move slowly and speak slowly are likely to be suffering from depression, not just extreme grief. Depression can make us slow down in just about every aspect of our lives and prevent us from being the people we were meant to be. It can get in the way of our progress and completely devastate our lives if it is left untreated.

Antidepressants are not generally the best route to deal with depression, especially if grief is the initial cause. Chances are high that depression that was brought on by grief needs to be treated internally and emotionally rather than with drugs that will help to get rid of the negative symptoms of depression. Sure, the symptoms being gone can be great, but the depression is much more likely to return if the root cause isn't unearthed and dealt with.

If you're grieving the death of a loved one or the loss of an important relationship, talking about that and allowing yourself to go through the different stages of grief, no matter how uncomfortable they may be, is the best way to help you to treat your depression and move forward in your life so that you will be able to continue making progress without being held back by negative feelings. Depression can ruin your life if you let it get too much control over yourself, so if you're able to really eradicate it from its source, then you're going to be much better equipped to embark upon the healing process.

Depression can leave us feeling despairing and lost, preoccupied with finding an end to the anguish that we're suffering through. This type of anguish is not typical of grief. Although grief can be very difficult to handle, it can also pave the way for much more painful experiences, such as depression that can leave us questioning our own worth and presence in the world. It is unbelievably important to seek support if you find yourself dealing with the feelings that depression can introduce to someone who is grieving. Although brief periods of depression are common during the five stages of grief, it's not normal for depression to last for weeks to months to years, and if it does persist in that degree then immediately seek support.

Otherwise, you may risk finding yourself stuck in a cycle of anguish and despair, and desperate for a way out of the negative feelings. Fortunately, there are some ways you can deal with depression. You can do your best to exercise every day. Exercise is mood enhancing and sends endorphins throughout your body that help you to feel better and stay positive. It even helps you to concentrate and retain information, which is especially helpful if you are suffering from depression. Depression and trauma can cause memory loss and difficulty with recalling things, so exercise can be very useful in this area.

Another thing you can do to combat depression is to seek support from friends and family members. Most of the time depression causes us to isolate ourselves, but in reality, being around people who care about us can make us feel a million times better. Begin a new hobby to get your mind off the difficult complexities of depression and help you to get a new lease on life.

However, if your depression is bad enough that you find yourself longing for death or blaming yourself for the loss you're experiencing, it's probably time to find a mental health professional that can help you to process your complicated feelings. The same is true if you find yourself unable to move through your daily life with the same ease and ability to function as you had before your loss, or you're finding it increasingly difficult to trust other people the way you once did. It is normal to feel strange after a loss, and we often find ourselves feeling numb and disjointed. However, if you feel this way longer than about a month, then it's time to bring your problems to somebody that can help you with them.

Depression can be a horrific way to spend your life, but if you're able to recognize the symptoms before they sink their claws into you then you will have the advantage. It is normal to feel all of these things to some degree during the grieving process, but when they begin to impact your life and prevent you from accomplishing the things that you once were able to do, then it's time for you to seek support. There is no shame in finding help. In fact, it's weaker to hide from your feelings and problems and drown them with alcohol and mind-numbing activities than it is to look your own issues straight in the eye and conquer them.

Depression isn't a joke. A lot of people make light of it because it's becoming such a common occurrence, but the fact is that it can change our lives and make them almost impossible to manage. If your grief has turned into clinical depression, seek support as soon as possible to take back control of your life.

Grief

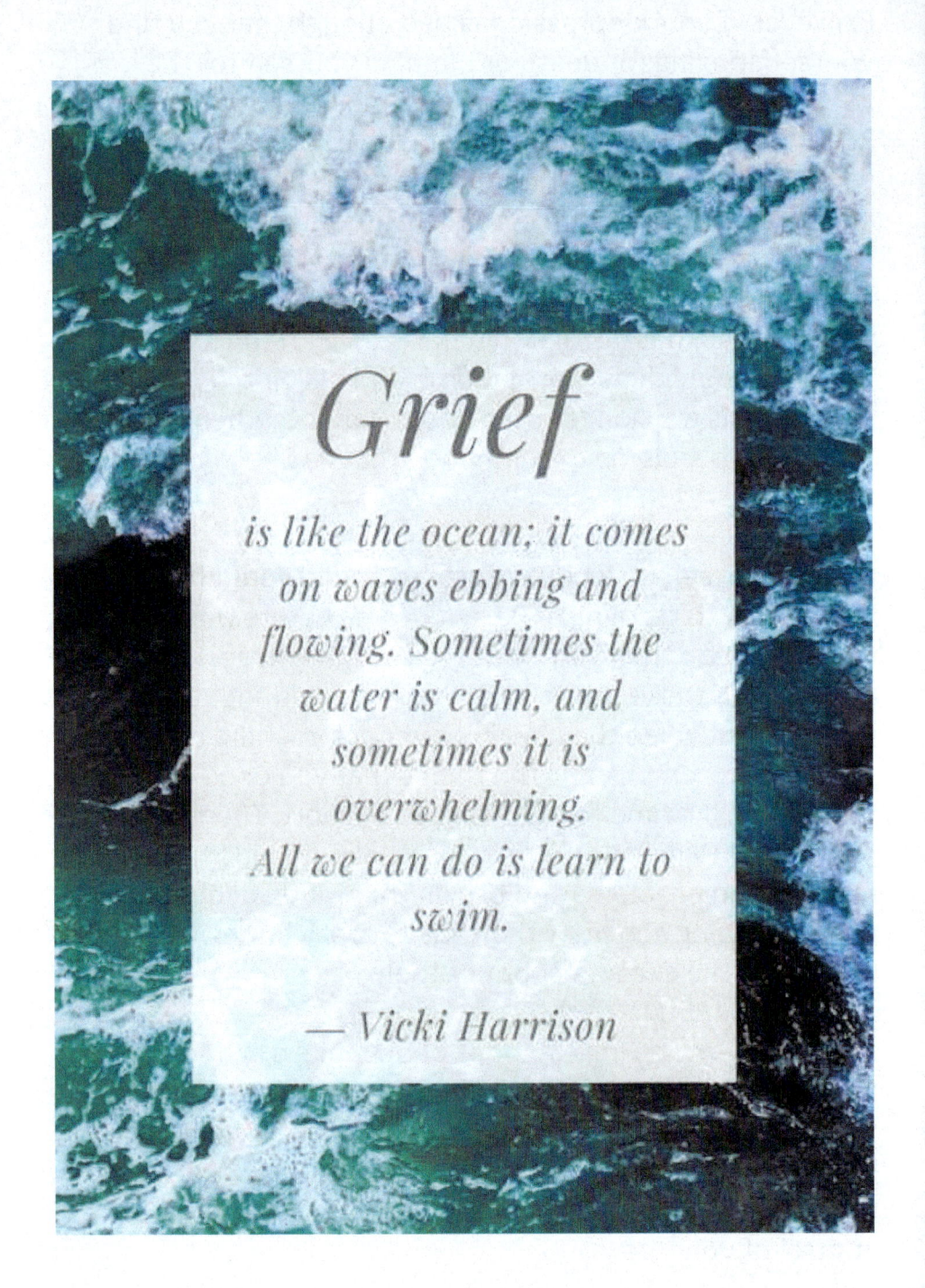

is like the ocean; it comes on waves ebbing and flowing. Sometimes the water is calm, and sometimes it is overwhelming. All we can do is learn to swim.

— Vicki Harrison

Chapter 8: Complications of Grief & How To Overcome Them

As you have probably gathered from the previous section, grief can quickly turn complicated. There is even a term for it: complicated grief. Complicated grief is a condition that some people find themselves in, which is characterised by a deep feeling of mourning and grief that completely consumes their lives. If you're going through the cycles of grief again and again without ever arriving at acceptance, then you may be experiencing complicated grief.

It is a very disruptive state to be in, and it can make every aspect of your life more difficult to manage. If you're living every day of your life like you're experiencing your loss in a new and fresh way, again and again, it can become impossible to maintain healthy relationships and accomplish goals that you might have had before you experienced your loss.

The sadness can be so overpowering that you begin to suffer from some very unique symptoms of grief. for example, you may begin to experience intrusive thoughts about the person that you lost that strike you with a painful force at unexpected moments during the day. It can leave you depleted as you long and yearn for the person that you lost. There are times you may find yourself confused and disoriented, looking around with a fiery purpose to find the person that you lost in the places you remember seeing them.

Some may even find comfort by imagining that the person they lost is actually not lost at all, but alive and well and still a part of their lives. Some people have a continuous sense of disbelief about the loss of their loved one and may refuse to accept the reality that the person they love so much is gone. This sense of denial and disbelief can be very profound and may lead to conflicts in relationships with people who are trying to help the person to understand that the loss is real and that coping is the only way to move forward.

Much like the stages of grief, complicated grief has many layers. Normal grief can involve anger, but complicated grief is more extreme than that, leading at times to rage and bitterness about the loss. People who experience this type of anger may feel furious at the person who left them or furious at anybody else who reminds them of the loss. Anger can be very hard to control, so outbursts of this nature can easily damage relationships.

Complicated grief can also involve depression and people who suffer from it may come to the false conclusion that without the person they lost, life is meaningless. It is common for people who experience complicated grief to feel empty and angry. Some people might even go to extreme lengths to avoid anything that reminds them of the person that they lost. It seems better in these cases not to think about the extreme pain of the loss and in effect, that person's existence in their life is all but erased.

The last thing you want is to erase the existence of a person who has passed away, but people who are so upset and devastated by a profound loss may do so without even meaning to. It can be so difficult to process the feelings they are dealing with, and so overwhelming, that it seems better not to feel anything about it at all. Unfortunately, being confronted with reminders of the loved one unexpectedly can leave us reeling when we have done our best to avoid any memories of the person we lost, and the acute pain felt in those moments is unbearable.

Complicated grief is unfortunately very common. We are often told that we need to get over our loss more quickly than we're ready to do, and if we listen to people who find it difficult to bear our emotional fragility and try to change the way we're grieving, it can lead to complications. Dealing with complicated grief is much more difficult than it is to deal with a normal, uninterrupted grieving process, and once it's noted that you may be dealing with the effects of complicated grief, the best source of action is to immediately seek support from a qualified professional that can help you to sort out these difficult emotions.

Complicated grief can leave us stuck and immobilized as we mourn the loss of our loved one with an acute sense of pain and longing. Most of the time, dealing with our grief in a healthy way will help us to avoid complicated grief, but there are times that a loss is just so difficult to bear that our minds are only doing their best to protect us from the pain and to compensate for the loss of the person we love. It can be a noble effort on our mind's part to defend against something we feel utterly vulnerable to, but in the long run, complicated grief can hurt us more than it helps us, no matter how comforting it might be to pretend the person we lost is still with us.

It takes a lot of strength to face this kind of loss, and if you're able to examine yourself and see symptoms of complicated grief and take the steps you need to get help for them, that means that you're brave enough to make it through this terrible tragedy and come out of it stronger than you ever could have imagined. Surviving a tragedy takes a toll on a person's body and mind, but it can also equip you with an inner strength that will help you to make it through every other situation you may face with a courage others can only hope to acquire.

Grief is like glitter.

You can throw a handful of it in the air, but when you try to clean it up, you will never get it all. Even long after the event, you will still find glitter tucked in the corners. It will always be there...somewhere.

Chapter 9: The Importance of Patience and Forgiveness

One thing most people forget during times of mourning and tragedy is to be patient with themselves. Most people assume that what they are feeling is wrong or inappropriate. Sometimes when we show emotion it can be very awkward, such as if we find ourselves breaking down into tears at a work meeting. These embarrassing situations can leave us feeling angry at ourselves for having any emotions and vulnerabilities, and it can make us feel impatient with ourselves. We might wish that we could just get over it already and continue on with life the way a normal person is supposed to live.

What we don't stop to realize is that we're exactly continuing on with life the way any normal person would when faced with the kind of loss that you're dealing with. You are not alone in your feelings of grief and sadness. In fact, there are probably thousands of people all over the world who are dealing with the same or similar symptoms of grief as you are right in the same moment. People die every day all over the world. Relationships end and tragedies and natural disasters occur.

No matter how embarrassing it may seem to be in an environment where people are not dealing with a similar tragedy, we're dealing with our sadness in the only way our bodies and minds know how to deal with them. It is perfectly normal to feel the way that you do. Don't try to rush your grieving process simply because it seems more convenient to do so. We need to give ourselves adequate time to begin to process the terrible events that are now the reality in our lives, and if we try to rush things, then it can become unhealthy for us. This can lead to complications in every aspect of our lives, including relationships with other people.

Do your best not to let your sense of propriety get in the way of a healthy grieving period. Most people take a couple of weeks off work or school so that they can begin to get a handle on their emotions in a reasonable time-frame without having to confront things they aren't ready to handle yet. Don't feel bad about taking some time to yourself, and don't feel bad if it doesn't turn out to be long enough for you. If you still feel like you're in the throes of grief, be patient with yourself. If other people don't understand it, that's lucky for them. But if they have ever suffered a loss like yours, then chances are high they will recommend the same thing.

One thing that can be very difficult during times of grief is the feeling of guilt that often accompanies times of loss. Most of us can't help but to search our minds for ways we could have acted better or prevented the terrible things from occurring. As humans, it's natural that we're always looking for answers and connections to events that may have no connection at all. But what we shouldn't do is assume there are connections when sometimes, a tragedy simply stands alone.

Sure, there may have been some unlikely way we could have intervened and changed the outcome of the tragedy, but the truth is that even if we could have done something, and it's unlikely that we could have, it didn't happen. Reality is still what it is. We weren't in the right place at the right time. We didn't have the power to change the outcome. And it's crucial that we forgive ourselves for that.

Even if we feel solely responsible for the outcome of a tragic event, it happened how it happened and there I sn't any way to go back in time and change it. Even if we did go back in time, the likelihood of our intervention changing the course of events is unbelievably slim. We can't blame ourselves for doing what we thought was the most important thing in the moment, and the person that we have lost most likely wouldn't want us beating ourselves up about it either.

One of the most crucial steps in overcoming grief is giving ourselves the permission to live again. If we join the ranks of the lost things that we're grieving, then the rest of our lives can quickly turn into a meaningless void. It's important to forgive ourselves for the things that we feel we had done wrong. We have to accept that we don't have the power to change the past and we have to be all right with that.

Who's to say that things would be better even if we did change the past? There is no knowing with things like this, and sometimes the tragedies in our lives help to shape the people that we are. Although it feels awful to suffer, tragedies often impact us in ways that give us more compassion and insight in the future.

We've got to be patient with ourselves as we grieve and forgive ourselves, both for being sad and having natural reactions to tragic events and for the things we worry we might have done differently. Although it is our natural response to try to find ways that we could change our circumstances, unfortunately during tragedies we rarely can. The only power we truly have is in how we perceive the situation and whether or not we allow ourselves to heal and move on as better for it, or we simply stay stuck in the pits of depression and eternal mourning.

We have the power to move on, but only if we're patient and forgiving with ourselves. Sure, you probably made a mistake or two during the course of the relationship with the tragedy you're facing, but one or two little mistakes probably hold no significant weight in the fate of that relationship. And whether it did or not, things happened how they did and now we have to face the future, not dwell in the past.

It can help to write down the things you feel were mistakes that may keep you from moving forward and practicing saying, "I forgive you," to each and every one. Whether you're saying that from your own perspective or if you can begin to imagine the person you feel you slighted saying it to you, this exercise can often help us to gain closure for the things that continue to haunt us.

You could practice writing in a journal about your daily experiences and feelings, and taking time to analyze which emotions are part of the stages of grief so that you may more easily forgive yourself for feeling angry and depressed.

It will help you to see your feelings as normal and natural, no matter what other people might say.

Don't rush yourself, even if others think it's time for you to move on. Cope with your loss as best you can, and if you feel it's taking too long or you're having a harder time than you should, don't hesitate to contact a trained professional who can help you to understand your complicated emotions.

But to face the future we have to forgive ourselves for any possible mistakes in the past, and we have to be patient as we go through the natural stages of grief that come with any significant loss. It will be a rollercoaster ride, and some days it may make you wonder whether or not you will be able to survive it, but you can and you will. All you have to do is be patient and understand that you have the power to face the future and move forward as a stronger person for it.

Whoever said that loss gets easier with time was a liar. Here's what really happens: The spaces between the times you miss them grow longer. Then, when you do remember to miss them again, it's still with a stabbing pain to the heart. And you have guilt. Guilt because it's been too long since you missed them last.

∞

KRISTIN O'DONNELL TUBB

Chapter 10: Seeing The Silver Lining and Learning To Appreciate Life

During times of grief, sometimes it can seem impossible that there will ever be another chance to view life in a positive way. The future can seem bleak and pointless when we're craving the comfort of a person or relationship that will no longer be there for us, and we forget that happiness and peace are still possibilities for us. We are stuck under a dark cloud of mourning that can make us feel depressed, isolated, and overwhelmed by sadness.

However, with every dark time comes a unique opportunity for the light to shine through, and it's up to us to learn how to spin the silver lining around each cloud. This can be easier to do with a positive support network of trusted friends and family members. But even if you feel entirely alone in this process, you can still find meaning in the darkest parts of life.

A lot of people take wisdom from their losses and tragedies that they begin to apply to their own lives. Many people suddenly realize the truth of their own mortality and how limited our time is on this earthly plain. It inspires many to live in the moment and waste no time at all, using every moment they've got to experience something new and wonderful or create something that can outlive them and sometimes even change the world.

Many of us assume that we'll have time in the future to do and say things to the people we love, but when you're faced with a tragedy that opens your eyes to the fact that tomorrow is not guaranteed, you can have more fulfilling relationships with those you care about without holding back the truth of how deeply you care about them.

No matter how tragic your loss may be, there's something to be gained. You may learn more about the way you approach relationships to others as you closely examine the way you relate to the person you lost. You can learn valuable insights about yourself and the world around you that can change the way you approach your life for the better. You may take others more seriously and become more compassionate or involved in a cause that's important. And maybe you will learn to manage your time more wisely now that you know just how valuable your time really is.

All of these are ways can be positively impacted by tragic events, and each of them will help us to move out of the grieving process and overcome the seemingly insurmountable pain of mourning. By allowing ourselves to take our mind out of the dark fog of sadness long enough to realize there are things of value to be taken from our experiences, we're able to have more control over our healing and move out of the dangerous state of mind that can lead to crippling depression and prolonged or complicated grief.

Instead of thinking about the terrible things associated with your loss, such as the suffering involved or the ways it could have changed, stop tormenting yourself and begin to think of the wonderful things that you can learn from your loss. You can learn how to be truly yourself. How to become an independent entity in the world capable of great things and making the changes that you need to make in order to live life exactly the way you want to live it. It can open your eyes to the suffering of others, and inspire you to dedicate your time to helping them in ways that only you ever could. There is hidden value in every experience, no matter how tragic, and opening your eyes through the pain can truly change your life.

It may also lead you to thinking about death in a practical sense. The truth is, if you are born, you are going to die. What we gain easily can be lost easily. And no matter who we love and what we've gained, we have to know exactly who we are with or without the people and things we care about. We have to know where we stand whether we're alone in a desert with no friends or possessions, or surrounded by the people we love. Grief should inspire us to examine who we truly are, right at the core, and provide us with the inspiration we need to become comfortable with ourselves and devoted to moving forward, no matter what else is going on in our lives. It is the attitude of a survivor.

With this mindset, you can begin to think about what will happen when you die yourself, and get your estate in order. You can speak to your family and friends about the things you wish to happen once you're gone, and feel inspired to think about the wisdom you'd like to impart upon the people you care about.

What would you like to tell everyone that, if you died tomorrow, you would regret keeping inside for so long? Use the experience to live in the moment and express your deepest truths to the world so that you may begin to take value from every relationship that you have.

It is more important than we might imagine to be able to survive these difficult experiences so that we can gain a sense of closure and peace, and when we do, we can begin to see that life, whether we suffer or not, is a beautiful thing full of opportunity. If we don't know how to celebrate life as we're living it, it gets squandered and wasted. What is most valuable during times of crisis is to remember that it's all a part of a much larger whole, and if we use our time wisely, we can impact the world around us in a much greater way than we might ever imagine.

Instead of wallowing in misery, especially if a loved one has passed away, we should allow ourselves to step outside of that sadness and think about the positive things that we're left with.

- What did we gain from the experience or relationship we had before we lost it?
- What can we learn?
- We should celebrate the lives of the people we lost and see what it is that we can learn from them.

When we examine the lessons we have learned, it can inspire us to live in the best way we know how every day so that we can keep the memory of the person we loved alive through our actions.

Celebrating life is the final step in overcoming grief. Whether we're going through a painful divorce or somebody we love has passed away, we can't think of life as the enemy or we'll never move on. It can seem impossible and unfair at times, but the truth is that life, even when sprinkled with tragedy, is a unique experience full of wonderful opportunities to connect with others and gain meaning out of even the darkest of times.

Life is what we make it, and experiencing grief is an opportunity to enrich our lives and become better people than we ever thought we could be. Instead of letting grief consume you, let it teach you. That is the best way to overcome.

Perhaps they are not the stars in the sky, but rather openings where our loved ones shine down to let us know they are happy

Final Thoughts and Further Insight

Overcoming grief is one of the most difficult things we are faced with in life, and because of this test of our mettle it can also be one of the most enriching.

Although it can be the darkest thing we have ever experienced, grieving is a normal and natural part of healing that can ultimately provide us with a new lease on life. As the old saying goes, it's always darkest before dawn. Although it can seem impossible to overcome, experiencing grief can help us to become better people.

Finding closure after a loss or a tragedy is a challenge, we are all met with at one time or another, and some people find that their grief becomes complicated or clouded by depression that can ruin their lives.

However, that doesn't have to be the case. If you surround yourself with a strong support network and you give yourself the time and patience you need to fully process your emotions, grieving can turn from the darkest time in your life to an opportunity to enrich your life in a way you might never have believed possible.

"There is no pain so great as the memory of joy in present grief."

AESCHYLUS

STORIES

DONNA - UK

My friend Aly and I were close for a long time. We met at pool and lived half a mile away from each other, so used to visit each other regularly and even when I moved away in the later years, we stayed in touch and saw each other when we could.

When Aly left us nearly 2 years ago, I got a message from her husband out of the blue to tell me she'd passed. She had been poorly but I didn't know how serious it had got. It wasn't necessarily her time to go. She was only still young and they think she had trouble with her breathing and had fallen out of bed. She died alone and was found by her husband. This really upset me a lot. It upsets me just writing it now. The thought of her possibly struggling and being alone in her final moments.

I didn't think it would hit me as hard as it did. But it did for a long while. Even still now, as I type this.

I was asked to speak at her funeral, which I did. And I don't really remember it but I know I did it. Not sure how.

I don't see a lot of our mutual friends now as I live quite a way away, but I do keep in touch with them all and Aly's husband Mark, so it's nice to chat about Aly and all the insanely funny times we had together. And to share photos of us all.

Aly would have wanted me to be happy. At any cost. And she would have wanted me to be the best mum I can be so I try hard to do this every day. And she'd laugh at me getting upset over writing this!

I find the positive by knowing she will be watching. She lives on in her son and I still hear her laugh and see her smile. She's still alive in my head and every now and again, she comes to see me in my dreams. That's always nice.

I keep the memory of Aly alive by speaking about her regularly, by speaking to her friends and family about her, and by remembering what a great friend she was and try to be the person she'd want me to continue to be.

Author:

It is difficult not to feel any emotion when the person you lose means so much to you.

Over time, the feeling of upset will subside and be replaced by joyous times as the way you have set it up with her husband, Mark, is a testament to you both.

Speaking to her friends and family about her is a great way for the slow release of pain that grief begins, to be replaced by happiness with her memories.

> "Grieving doesn't make you imperfect. It makes you human."
>
> **SARAH DESSEN**

SANDI RICHARDS - UK

Jim was strong, grounded, fun loving and principled. He completely underrated himself. He was an epic problem solver, could turn his hand to anything and soaked up knowledge. Typical Jim projects: a homemade snow plough built out of an old lawn mower and some gas bottles, a ride on lawn mower from a broken plastic chair, wheelbarrow and an old push lawn mower. He helped me renovate my house to a beautiful holiday let and now I'm selling it with a big profit. I wish he was with me to enjoy the fruits of his labour.

I was going to retire this year so that we could chill using the income from the holiday let. He had just bought a little fishing boat, and even though I don't fish, I can't bear to let the boat go. It is a symbol of what the next stage of our life together was going to be.

The effect of his death on me has been catastrophic. I've lost myself. I don't know who I am anymore. I've stopped participating in most things I used to do: volunteer groups, community groups, landmark assisting - I've stopped it all. I have a new interest, my grandchild who is 14 months old now. I look after him 2 days a week so that my daughter can work and that's the only thing I really want to do. I am still working the other 3 days, mostly to give me something to do.

I don't really see the point in anything. I look after Wes to support Bella and it occupies my mind. But I worry that I'm just enabling them to keep on the same hamster wheel that got me nowhere. I was about to achieve what I've been aiming for, (after years of working hard to be the best I can be and make a difference in the world); an income that allows me to live, volunteer and chill and the person I was going to do that with has gone. I look around and the world is still a shitty place. My efforts have made no difference. We are manipulated and controlled by a few with all the money. Our lives are not our own. Our decisions are meaningless.

I know I'm depressed and I suspect it's not just Jim's death. The covid debacle has brought me face to face with how manipulated and controlled we are and how meaningless my attempts to make a difference have been. The two things together have stopped me in my tracks. I'm now rudderless and have lost the comfort of my soulmate to see me through. Jim used to say 'Find your Centre'. I don't even know where to look now.

Friends and family are helping loads by keeping in touch, not letting me sink into misery. Being at my daughters half the week gives me some structure. When I'm home friends check in, make sure I'm eating, provide company. They support me with checking on the house while I'm away. I'm lucky to have so many friends around, but sometimes the advice and wish to help is overwhelming. I have to split my time between different friends so that they all get a chance to be with me and do their bit.

Jim would want me to get on with my life. One of his expressions was 'shit happens' and this is just one of those things. I do feel I'm dishonouring him by not moving forward, but that doesn't seem to be enough to get me out of this rut. I think the bottom line is, I just don't care anymore. I don't want to be here, but I can't leave because I would never do that to my daughter, so I'm stuck. The only way I can handle it is to keep my mind occupied with day- to-day things, or Netflix, and not engage with all the crap that's going on in the world.

I think about Jim all the time, and talk about him. I don't have to actively keep his memory alive. I have day dreamed some of the trips we were planning. We've been on a fishing trip, been to Berlin, stayed in a log cabin. All in my day dreams. The dreams do seem to have a life of their own. I have an image of him cooking breakfast in the log cabin and it seems totally real, more like a memory than an invention.

I sometimes think he speaks to me through Wes, my grandson. They never actually met but I do wonder if they are in touch. Strange things occasionally happen in Wes's room and I can feel really close to him when I'm looking into Wesley's dozing eyes. Or maybe that's just the gorgeous feeling of a baby falling asleep in your arms!

I haven't found many positives in Jim's death. Mostly it seems all wrong. I probably am spending more time with my daughter and her family than I would have, which I love and I'm closer to his son but not much else. It helps knowing how much I was loved and I wouldn't forfeit that.

I doubt that I will ever be me again, and I do miss who I was. It doesn't seem like there is any way back now and I'm not ready to move forward.

Grief seems to be an experience of extremes. I am shocked at how much it has derailed me. I have great admiration for everyone that has dealt with the loss of a loved one.

Thank you for the opportunity to express myself.

Author:

This is a familiar place for most of those who have lost someone. Feelings of guilt, anguish, continuous over thinking and being lost now that the person is no longer here.

As Jim would say "shit happens" but there is no dishonour in not moving forward. Everyone deals in grief in different ways and at their own pace.

There may be things that you want to say to Jim as an unfinished conversation. You could write a letter to Jim explaining what is going on for you regarding his passing and also anything else you would like to say to him. Go to a quiet place and read it to him as if he is standing in front of you. If this is emotionally challenging then having your daughter and grandson present, will help.

A possible way forward for yourself could be to create a purpose in your life or to reconnect to what yourself and Jim were up to. Go to the places that you had planned to go to. Speak to your daughter about the memory of Jim, speaking to people who knew Jim will help.
It's great that you have people to look out for you but you need to look out for you.

Knowing which stage of grief you are presently in (see the 5 Stages of Grief above) will help give you some solace, peace of mind, structure and guidance to where you are and what is too come.

So all may not be lost....

> "You can't truly heal from a loss until you allow yourself to really feel the loss."
>
> **MANDY HALE**

BOG FRANCI - UK

My mother. She run away from home...not sure why. But nearly sure that something was extremely wrong as we never had a real contact with her family. Only some sisters and one brother, who later killed himself.

We were two children. She made my sister with a guy who never recognized her and what mother told us...he tried to kill my sister when she was baby.

And she had me 6 years after my sister. And my father died 2 weeks before I arrived...she was working like a cleaner in the municipality house...every day. She was working afternoon shifts so we only see her on Saturdays and Sundays...all other days we spend with caretakers...she was extremely angry on the system especially after she retired. But after I done the Landmark forum...we become connected like never before...

I was ready and comfortable when she left as she was in the caring home few years before and become completely out of the world with dementia...but we were still connected somehow and for me was relieved when she died. And I am sure that she was happy too. She constantly told me that she would like to go as she did not have anything else here to do! And I was happy too...I had a speech on her grave and i become present to everything what she done and to all the sacrifices she made that we are here...living!

In the beginning when I start traveling around the world...she was upset and angry. She said: "If you go...you are never welcome here again!" I was 14!

But I was more than welcome when I come back as she slowly understands that I am living her dreams...

We celebrate new births and we all know that we will all die from the day we are born. Why we would not celebrate death too? I think that we should enjoy every moment with loved ones...and if we are not attached to them but we really love them then is the moment when they died the best moment of our life...as we know that their job is finished! Moment for celebration and joy!

With the monument on the graveyard...visiting every now and then. I put photos on fb...mostly on the day she died. And a lot of times she come on my mind when I need to do something or when I don't know how to do it...I remember her advice in my head! And sometimes I just light the candle for her...

Author:

**It's great to be present to the sacrifices that our parents did to then bring us into this world. They did this for us.
You may have a great point there, to not only celebrate when someone is born but to also celebrate their life once they pass away!!
Parents are our teachers in life and you always remember their teachings.**

"Grief is a curious thing, when it happens unexpectedly. It is a band–aid being ripped away, taking the top layer off a family. And the underbelly of a household is never pretty, ours no exception."

JODI PICOULT

ANNA - GERMANY

Can you tell me about your loved one? Maria is my first daughter and she was diagnosed in the womb as quite ill. We had an operation to try save her, which seemed to be successful but a day later, on Christmas Eve, we got the news her heart had stopped beating. She had Turners Syndrome. She was still born on Christmas morning 2016. The "long version" of her story is shared here if it's of any interest for the grief community!

https://www.storiesfromthetrenches.org/blog/2017/5/23/gone-ahead

In 2020 we lost little "Erin" to miscarriage at about 9 weeks. We never found out if it was a boy or a girl, this little baby is buried with its sister Maria. The shock and disbelief that we would bury another child is still VERY present today. It's unbelievable but to fill out the whole story, in addition to child loss within our immediate family, since Maria died, we have also lost many nieces and nephews: an ectopic pregnancy, a lost twin, my sister in laws girl was stillborn girl at 37 weeks and my brother's daughter little Rosie was stillborn at 41 weeks.

What has been the effect on you? Quoting from the blog entry above, although it was written after Marias death, it has been the same effects after losing Erin as well. "My faith was shattered, and I no longer wanted to live. I struggled to distinguish jealousy from sadness as our friends' bumps and babies continued to grow. I struggled to understand that my husband grieved just as deeply, albeit differently. I hated my body, missing my bump while trying to lose weight. I was so scared that our families would talk about other grandchildren and great-grandchildren but not about our Maria.

People who had been there for us during the pregnancy were now resorting to strained small talk or painful platitudes." Most of those effects I still feel. Through a lot of grief counselling I have managed to restore my faith in God again. For quite some time I still had traumatic nightmares about baby loss, these have eased up in the last year I would say.

There have also been the "secondary" losses as they are sometimes called - for example; Relationships with family and friends (people who cannot be with your grief), celebrations (Christmas has become the hardest time of the year for me), pregnancies (both your own after loss, crippled with fear, and dealing with this fear for others as well). And just the nightmare of that seemingly small talk question "How many kids do you have"… do I deny my angels and protect this person from the reality that is baby loss? Or do I tell them and watch them turn purple and gulp not knowing what to say?! And then sometimes, they tell you they lost babies too, and you make a new friend….

How can your friends around you help? Say their names, acknowledge me as a mother of four children even if two are invisible to you! Remember them with me, remember significant dates, understand that some seasons and celebrations are hard for me and I need space to cry and grieve. How would she/he want you to move forward? I remember struggling with the idea of laughing, listening to music or dancing ever again after the first trauma of loss.

A fellow loss father said to me, living children are happy when they see their parents happy, how about we imagine our children in heaven looking down smiling when we smile. Also, **Nora McInerny's book** "its ok to laugh, crying is cool too" was a great access to this idea of "moving forward". I remember to this day the first time I laughed after these losses, and the people who helped me to laugh again.

It's not that I consider laughing signifying "being over anything" but it was a big step in allowing myself to live with the grief. It never goes away, I never stop thinking about them, but, and this also was from grief counselling and Nathalie Himmelrich's writings, I try to let some memories bring me peace and not anxiety.

For example, when my mind races and remembers being handed my dead daughter and I remember the horrors of the hospital, I try to practice instead remember seeing her on the ultrasound happily playing with her toes instead. It's an ongoing effort though and often doesn't work for me! How do you find the positive in all of this? I don't believe in "life gives you lemons make lemonade", babies die and it sucks and people hate to talk about it! I met some wonderful souls through my grief, yes, but none of us see these friendships as anything that makes our losses "worthwhile".

My stance on this at the moment, from a christian perspective, is simply that life down here is the back of the tapestry, it makes no sense why God allows such horrific things to happen, but when we get to Heaven someday, we will see the front of the tapestry, and all the "mess" will make sense. I cannot survive any day that I lose this trust in God. How do you keep the memory of your loved one alive? I am very much a "grave person" so we visit the grave at least once a week.

I buy little things for the children at Christmas, Easter etc. to decorate the grave, and flowers or something on their anniversaries and due dates. I have a corner in the living room dedicated to their memories with photos, statues, memory boxes, teddies things like that. And some photos dotted around the house. Until the living children came along, I always wore a locket with a photo in it, but the wee ones tend to pull too much at necklaces so that's resting for now until they are older! When we write to family, we often sign the cards with things like "with Maria and Erin in our hearts" or "remembering Maria and Erin".

Since having the living siblings, we always share with them about their siblings in heaven, my daughter is now 4 and it's a great comfort to us to hear her say things like "I have a big sister, Maria. She's waiting for me in heaven". And we talk about them. My close friends "get this". Anyone who doesn't or starts to act a bit odd when I refer to my "angel babies", I honestly have distanced myself from.

Author:

It seems that you are in a great place now.

I can't imagine what it must be like to lose a child as a parent.

"Tears shed for another person are not a sign of weakness. They are a sign of a pure heart."

JOSE N. HARRIS

CINDY – AUS

Maree Matic

Can you tell me about your loved one?

I met Maree circa 2003 in a job interview; it was the most unusual interview. The whole team got to meet me and collectively decide who the best fit for the team.

She and I just clicked & our conversation was flowing to the point of completing each other's sentences.

I got the job due to her big mouth (talkative nature & great negotiation skills; she should have been a lawyer).

During our time in this job; we communicated well, laughed lots; helped each other and the team and team leader got distracted by our high achieving distractive work. They separated us in the office.

We couldn't stop talking and profoundly we were extremely productive.

Maree had a really unfortunate circumstances in her life; an abusive father, a mother who died of cancer; a brother who was alcoholic and was assaulted that year by a taxi driver. She rolled with life's punches but not really dealing with it all.

Our friendship continued while she changed career, moved house (now we lived 3 suburbs away).

She travelled abroad to work in an orphanage in Thailand for over 12 months.

All she ever wanted to do in this life; is help people, save children, inspire the work to heal from their trauma's. Dealing with her own pains was difficult and swept under the rug with a smile.

She would talk to anyone and never cared to give all her money to the begger's on the street. She often believed in giving without judgment and the fact that person is worse of than her.

She loved everyone and every animal with every fibre of her being. She would avoid crushing ants as she walked on the pavement too.

She inspires loving everyone the same unconditionally.

Her passing in 2014 was one of the most challenging in my life. She discovered breast cancer early 2013 and refused to operate or do anything other than approach it holistically. As the lump grew and the pain was extreme; she accepted chemo, then radiation, then chemo; then finally early 2014, an operation.

The operation was cancelled with the news the cancer spread to the liver & lungs. The journey was a constant losing battle; I don't think she wanted to really heal for the fear and trauma she felt from her mother's death 20 years earlier and her brother 2 years (2011) earlier from a drug and alcohol overdose.

This woman was adamant that the healing would just happen and she would recover. She was stubborn and very fearful. She had unresolved trauma that was way too difficult to digest, confront or dissolve. She tried to do the healing work.

It was the end of line with the doctors as this cancer metastasised to a triple negative, a genetic mutation and the spread of the cancer was not helping.

She entered palliative care only to pass away less than two weeks.

She left a whole in my heart.

She was the Soul Sister (the older sister I never had).

What has been the effect on you?

This woman taught me a lot about myself; got me to think beyond my limited beliefs. She was someone who championed me and celebrated my small and big wins in life. She celebrated the things I did even though she struggled to change so many things in her life. She was never envious or jealous. She taught me to be courageous, do things even though it scares me, believe in my gut instincts; but that voice was gone now!

Her passing left me to fend for myself, feeling lost and forcing me to reflect on fear and how to overcome it.
It was time to stand on my own!

How can your friends around you help?

My friends were helpful; some kept me busy with activities, weekend away trips; and held space for me to grieve. It took me about 3 months to shift the deeper part of grief that resided heavily in my heart. I found the social balance has to change too now. I felt somewhat lost and demanded more from my friends, until I reached a new equilibrium within me.

How would she/he want you to move forward?

I am sure; she wanted me to do all things I was scared to do & go beyond myself. I often feel her pushing me along even to do the things she was scared to do.

She would want me happy, content and courageous at every turn.

She would want me to drop all the baggage that may have held me up in life from progress.

How do you find the positive in all of this?

Moving on with hope always... I took one step at a time; then I would run along with life and on occasion reflect on a conversation with her and say "if you could be here right now witnessing how the world has changed as you talk about", you'd be so impressed".

She had a vision of change and everyone coming from a heart space and higher consciousness. Right now, people are becoming more aware of themselves, their surroundings and assessing their values as well. We talked for hours about these changes; we are experiencing now. We talked a lot about quantum energy and how it changes the world; we are now experiencing it all now.

How do you keep the memory of your loved one alive?
Her memory is always with me. I celebrate her birthday; remember her on the day she passed and often see photos of her on past Facebook posts.

In the healing process, I kept seeing heart and butterflies which is a reminder of loving her and feeling that she is actually watching over us (the butterfly).

In my home, have these items as ornaments to constantly remind me of her when I need to reflect. Our mutual friends and I still message and speak of her too often. Her memory is alive and it made moving on easier.

Her desire on this earth was to reach millions of people with the message of love, self-love, healing etc; but what she didn't know that she affected people in millions of ways.

That was her legacy!

Vale "Biserka (pearl) Maree Matic"

Author:

Sometimes when we hear bad news, it is easy to shut down our communication to our friends and family as we don't want to burden them with our problems and want to do it on our own.

There is no shame in sharing what is going on for you as you may then have a good friend to help you in your journey to recovery.

Having visual triggers like the butterfly ornaments and celebrating the persons birthday are positive things to do to aid in the healing process.

"The reality is that you will grieve forever. You will not 'get over' the loss of a loved one; you'll learn to live with it. You will heal and you will rebuild yourself around the loss you have suffered. You will be whole again but you will never be the same. Nor should you be the same nor would you want to."

ELISABETH KUBLER-ROSS AND DAVID KESSLER,
ON GRIEF AND GRIEVING

MICKY T – UK

Grief cuts at different levels and my dads passing was the most devastating. His passing was quite sudden and unexpected so we went from having a normal day to rushing about, phone calls, hospital visits, discussion amongst family on the way forward and who could help in different ways. Who should be told what! The grandchildren, how do you tell them that he wasn't well, that he might not make it, that they might not see him again, where he was going, why was he going.

What happens next. The closer siblings and family are aware of everything and we try to support one another. Even after he passed, brothers and sisters were there for each other, you speak about what has happened, you talk about the present and you talk about the future. We all knew that person, what he stood for, his values. We also knew that the loss of him would happen one day and it's something that you do prepare yourself for but you also never look forward to that day and it comes as quite a shock with the suddenness of events.

With a long time illness, you can prepare yourself in a gradual way as we all know one day it will happen. But even with the suddenness, close family step up to help you as you help them.

Friends are also there offering help in any way possible but I always found that although their offers are greatly appreciated and heartfelt, moments like that are somewhat private and family are more understanding in your own private feelings.

My dad would never want us to be unhappy and he would want us to live life to the full and achieve our dreams and to be happy. His last song was Frank Sinatra's 'My Way' and it was appropriate to the way he lived 'a life that's full'. Nobody wants to lose someone they love but at some stage of life its inevitable and it hurts.

Time will always be a great healer and that love will never die, it doesn't even get pushed to the back burner as every day, a thought, a memory will arise and reignite the memory. I have a picture on my wall at the bottom of the stairs that I see every morning and sometimes I tuck my betting slip and lottery ticket under the back of it to look for that bit of luck, but unfortunately, he was an awful gambler and that makes me smile, I still trust him and speak to him as I place that ticket there lol. The positives I find from his passing is that we are not here for a long time, just try to have a good time, be nice to people. Look for the good not the negatives and pass that smile, that good feeling around to the people near you.
God bless you dad, Love you forever. Michael

Author:

Death is inevitable unfortunately and potentially imminent especially when a parent has a long term illness. Thoughts of them passing away come into your mind more and you mentally prepare for them not being here for the future. So every moment with them is precious.

Having a photo of them at the bottom of the stairs is brilliant as it will be a constant reminder of your dad and if 1 bet can come in, with his prayers, then woo hoo :-)

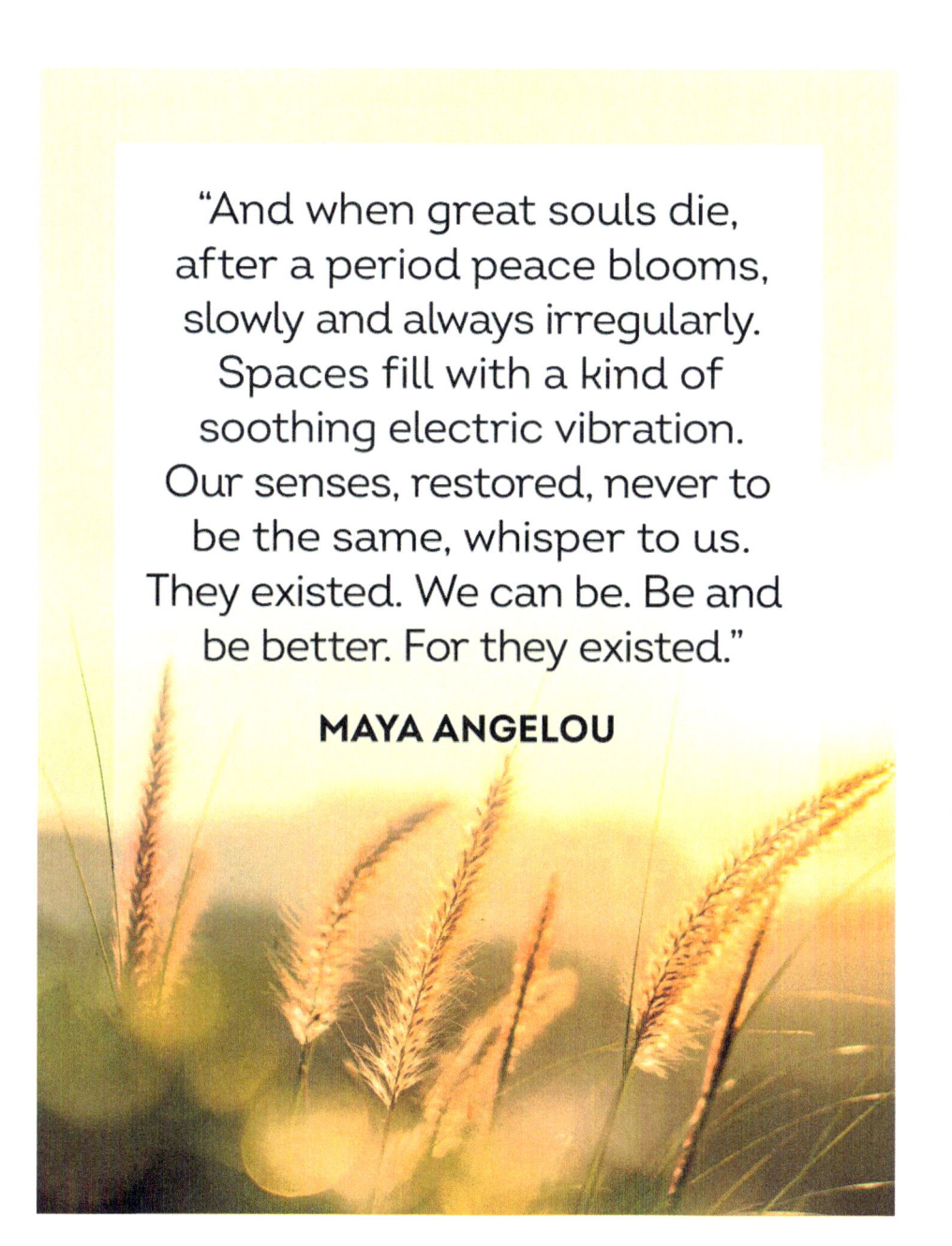

"And when great souls die, after a period peace blooms, slowly and always irregularly. Spaces fill with a kind of soothing electric vibration. Our senses, restored, never to be the same, whisper to us. They existed. We can be. Be and be better. For they existed."

MAYA ANGELOU

MERRICK - UK

So about 6 days after my 16th birthday my mum passed away. I remember it being a huge shock at the time because we were never told just how ill my mum was. It was kept quiet. Maybe she didn't want us to know because she didn't want to worry us, but certainly the word cancer was never ever mentioned. As you can imagine at the time it turned my whole world upside down.

For perhaps the first time in my life it made me realise how quickly things can change and how precious life is. One minute everything is 'normal', the next minute the rug is pulled from under your feet and the path you were on takes an entirely different direction.

Initially, I was just angry at everyone and anything. I couldn't understand why this had happened to my mum. She was the kindest nicest person in the world so the fact that this had happened to her just didn't seem fair to me. That anger was always just under the surface and started to spill out into areas of my life. If I wasn't challenging those around me, I was pushing people away. It was a really tough stage in my life as I tried to come to terms with it all. The thing is my mum was the glue of the family and her not being there left a hole. Luckily, I had good friends around me who helped drag me from my darkness. My school friends were amazing in that respect.

I remember there were about 6 in particular who put into a collection for flowers for my mum's funeral. I've always kept the card that came with the flowers because it just meant so much to me at the time. It just helped having their support and people to talk to about how I was feeling. They made allowances for me when I would take things out on them. They understood how hard it was for me and they never took it personally.

I don't remember when, but at some point, I decided to refocus my energy. Growing up mum used to say "no matter how bad you think things are going for you, realise that there are people who are worse off". Appreciate what you've got and help others. I've tried to live my life by that and a lot of who I am today can be traced back to the values my mum installed in me.

The biggest driving force for me though was the promise I made to her. When I went to the hospital to see her for the last time, I leaned over to kiss her on her cheek and told her that I would make her proud. It's helped push me to where I am now and it's definitely because of her.

I feel like I've fulfilled that promise. At the same time, you have to be mindful of the fact that you can't let your past dictate your future. That's not what she would have wanted. She would want me to live in the moment and enjoy life and to move on. That was just the type of person she was. She wouldn't want me to let what happen take over my life.

It doesn't mean she is forgotten though. I always light a candle on my mum's birthday or on the anniversary of when she left us, and have a glass of Baileys because that was my mum's favourite drink. She lives on within me and the rest of my family and has shaped our lives in ways that I couldn't have imagined.

Author:

When a parent passes, we go through all sorts of emotions like anger, guilt and regret. It is important to just be with what is going on and try to articulate how you are feeling along the way. Communication is key.

Do something that they used to like doing as a way of remembering and live your life the way they would want you too.

The memory never goes away, its just that you can't physically touch or hug them.

"To live in hearts we leave behind is not to die."

THOMAS CAMPBELL

ANTHONY - UK

First, it was my mum then 3 and a half years later, my father whom I was a full-time carer for, passed away (dementia). When my mother passed, I was on my own and was diagnosed with MS. I never had time to mourn her death which wasn't healthy. It was so bad that the GP, signed me off from being my dad's carer but I still went round every morning at 8am and staying every weekend.

I lost my way in life as I used to go out and laugh and joke all the time. I kept a couple of close friends but the rest vanished but trying to put a brave face on but it isn't always as easy as it seems. Talking to friends made me feel like I was a burden so I stopped talking to them.

My mum or dad wouldn't have wanted me to have hurt so bad and mum would have wanted me to get my life on track again which is easier said than done. I go to the cemetery every weekend, on birthdays and anniversaries. Sometimes, my youngest and I go twice a week.

Author:

Give yourself permission to mourn your mothers death properly. I don't know what this would look like but the first step could be to write a letter to your mum explaining everything you ever wanted to say to her and in her passing.

Go to a quiet place and read it out to her as if she is standing opposite you listening.

Have friends and family around you to talk to them of how each of you are coping and share your experience.
We all grieve in different ways and over various time scales, so having this structure in place will ease the pain.

The purpose of this book is to have you look at what stage of grief you are at and that there is a way forward in following the steps above to get to a place where you are not affected mentally and emotionally with your parents passing.

"Never. We never lose our loved ones. They accompany us; they don't disappear from our lives. We are merely in different rooms."

PAULO COELHO

My Story.

Last week, late June 2022, at the time of writing this, it was the 3rd anniversary of my mother's passing.

After stumping her toe, we took mum to the hospital and the doctor told us that she had low blood supply to her left leg. After further tests, she only had 8% function of both her kidneys. They wanted to keep her in for observation.

Two days later, the hospital said that they wanted to put her on a dialysis machine where she would need to come to the hospital every other day for dialysis. Go home and then come back the following day. I thought, at least she would be able to come home every other day, but because of her condition, she never left the hospital.

Before she went on dialysis, we would speak to her and she was coherent, mum would laugh and have jokes with us but once the dialysis started, it's a bit like the lights are on but nobody is home!! All of the joy had just washed away. The doctors proceeded to tell us that they wanted to amputate her leg. Mum was already causing a fuss with the way her toe was and we as a family decided that "hell no are you amputating our mother's leg".

The doctors then spoke to us about DNR, which is "Do Not Resuscitate" they had given her some morphine to ease the pain but she was still hurting as we looked at her. I asked them what "resuscitate" involved and they said "what we do is we crack open the rib cage and with gloves on, we manually massage the heart to make it beat" It was a very tough decision to take but we didn't want her to go through an undignified procedure as she is our mother, so we as a family, decided that when she was ready to leave, she would.

I saw her on the Thursday evening, went home and she passed away on Friday early morning.

She was like a buddy to me and we would share jokes and laughs.

I would tickle her and she would listen to my stories and what was going on in my life. I have learnt my humanity and humility through my mother. Even now, as I read this back, I am smiling as I think about her.

As I'm a chauffeur driver, the following weeks were very difficult, as I would think about her all the time or what she would be like with my new story and how she would respond to it. To help me, I would have conversations with riders in the car, who would eventually speak to me and tell me that one of their parents had died and how they were feeling. Sometimes in the car, both myself and the rider would cry and remember the good times of our parents.

Mum and dad were married for over 50 years and when mum passed, dad was left on his own and a carer would come in every day, twice a day, to make sure he had his meals prepared. I would go and see him on a Tuesday evening to a Thursday afternoon to make sure his medicine is correct; it has been re-ordered; encourage him to get out of the house and go for a walk with me; to speak to his friends on the street and get some fresh air.

We grew very close and last October 2021, unfortunately due to illness he passed away. I am grateful to have had the opportunity to spend that year and a half to get to know my dad over again. These are memorable moments that I have spent with him since the 2 1/2 years that my mother had passed.

Speaking to riders in the car has really helped myself and the riders come to terms with losing both parents or a parent, to be empathetic with each other, to listen and also sometimes to let the rider speak so that they can be heard because it is very difficult for friends of a person who has lost a parent to be there for them.

They don't share the same experience so I suggest that they just be there for them in whichever way they can and tell their friend "Whatever you need, I am here for you". When they are ready to talk about what has happened to them, they will communicate. There is no timeline in this.

This is when I came up with the idea of writing a book because there is no real step-by-step process to help somebody along or even hold them by the hand and guide them through what they are going through. A positive way of coping with both parents passing, is to always remember them on their birthdays and anniversaries. Remember the good times, remember what they used to teach you, their sayings and mottos and their humour.

In my research for the book, I interviewed riders in the car by asking them questions about their deceased parent. With their permission, I asked them if I could record the answers to some questions and if they were happy for me to do so, then I would add their answers into a story for the book.

For those that have shared their story with me, I will give them a copy of the book for free to help them with their journey. I also asked friends if they were okay to share their experience. Some said yes and they also would get a free copy of the book so I began the research finding out what the five stages of grief are.

Incorporating the riders and friends stories into the book at the end, followed by the authors thoughts. I wanted to make this book a bit different from others.

The purpose of this book is to hold your hand and walk you through each step, firstly locating where you are in the five stages and what is the next stage to come.

Also, giving handy hints like, if you wanted to say something to your parents but you never got the chance to. To then have peace within yourself after somebody who has died because what we normally tend to do is we go into the blame game. "Why didn't I do more" "I should have spent more time with them" Sometimes, remorse will set in, where you will look for a quick fix.

"Pills"
"Alcohol"
"Drugs"

These are short term fixes unfortunately, which can lead to addictive tendencies and then dependance. So you have to be careful!! The smoother transition is to work from the inside.

'Feelings'
'Communication'
'Acceptance'
'Reflection'

I hope that this book will help those who have unfortunately lost a parent to come to terms with their passing and move on as their parents would have wanted them to live an amazing life, be happy and comfortable that they have lost someone very special.

What I miss about my parents is the physicality; touching them, hugging them and having jokes and laughter with them.

The memories will always live on and will bring a smile to my face on their birthdays but also bring a tear to my eyes RIEP Mum and Dad.

I love you both very much and miss you all the time.

DEDICATED TO MUM & DAD xx